IRISH CROWN JEWELS THEFT

BY ASHLEY GISH

Apex is distributed by North Star Editions:
sales@northstareditions.com | 888-417-0195

Produced for Apex by Red Line Editorial.

Photographs ©: Historic Collection/Alamy, cover, 9; History and Art Collection/Alamy, 1, 7; Shutterstock Images, 4–5, 12, 13, 14–15, 21, 25, 26, 29; iStockphoto, 10–11, 22–23; Bain News Service/George Grantham Bain Collection/Library of Congress, 16–17, 24; Frank Hurley/ Underwood & Underwood/Library of Congress, 18; Chronicle/Alamy, 20

Library of Congress Control Number: 2022911844

ISBN
978-1-63738-434-3 (hardcover)
978-1-63738-461-9 (paperback)
978-1-63738-513-5 (ebook pdf)
978-1-63738-488-6 (hosted ebook)

Printed in the United States of America
Mankato, MN
012023

NOTE TO PARENTS AND EDUCATORS

Apex books are designed to build literacy skills in striving readers. Exciting, high-interest content attracts and holds readers' attention. The text is carefully leveled to allow students to achieve success quickly. Additional features, such as bolded glossary words for difficult terms, help build comprehension.

TABLE OF CONTENTS

CHAPTER 1

THE THEFT

On July 6, 1907, a messenger came to Dublin Castle. He brought a gold collar. It would be stored at the castle.

The Bedford Tower at Dublin Castle had a safe to keep jewels that were used for special events.

Sir Arthur Vicars was in charge of the castle's treasure. He sent someone to put the collar in the castle's safe. But the safe was unlocked. And the Irish Crown Jewels were missing.

A SPECIAL SET

The jewels belonged to the Order of St. Patrick. That was a group of aristocrats. Its leader wore the jewels at special events. They included a badge, a star, and gold collars.

The leader of the Order of St. Patrick was known as the Grand Master.

People had last seen the jewels on June 11. They were stolen sometime after that.

FAST FACT

The missing jewels had nearly 400 gems. Today, they'd be worth more than $4 million.

The Irish Crown Jewels were decorated with many emeralds, rubies, and diamonds.

CHAPTER 2

THE INVESTIGATION

The Dublin police investigated. The safe's lock wasn't damaged. So, the thief likely had a key.

Dublin Castle had many guards. It was hard to break into.

The safe was kept in the castle's library.

The thief also left clues. Two doors in the castle were unlocked. And a ribbon was left in the safe. The thief had removed it from the jewels.

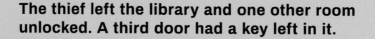

The thief left the library and one other room unlocked. A third door had a key left in it.

The Bedford Tower was near a gate that was one of the main entrances to Dublin Castle.

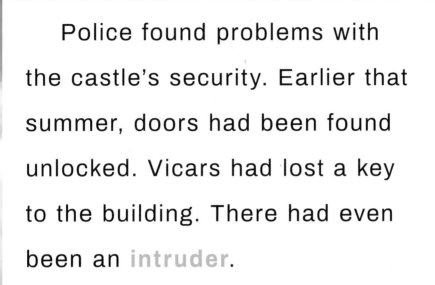

Police found problems with the castle's security. Earlier that summer, doors had been found unlocked. Vicars had lost a key to the building. There had even been an intruder.

NOT VERY CAREFUL

Vicars had known about the security problems. But he hadn't done much about them. And he sometimes showed the jewels to his friends.

CHAPTER 3

SEVERAL SUSPECTS

Police thought the thief was someone who worked at the castle. Vicars was one suspect. But he didn't have a clear motive.

Vicars's job involved keeping the castle's records and treasure. He was known for being detailed and picky.

Francis Shackleton was another. Shackleton was in debt. He wasn't in Dublin on July 6. But he could have had help.

FAST FACT

Francis Shackleton's brother, Ernest, was an explorer. He needed money to pay for his trips.

◄ **Ernest Shackleton (right) was famous for exploring Antarctica.**

The jewels went missing right before King Edward VII visited Dublin for a world's fair.

People had other theories. Irish groups disliked the British king. They could have taken the jewels to make him look bad. Other people said the monarchy planned the theft.

UNSAFE SAFE

One time, Vicars's friend Lord Haddo stole the safe's key. He took the Irish Crown Jewels as a joke. He mailed them back to Vicars.

Several staff members had keys to the Bedford Tower.

CHAPTER 4

STILL A MYSTERY

Dublin's police never arrested anyone for the theft. Chief Inspector John Kane of Scotland Yard came to help. He wrote a report saying who he thought was guilty.

Scotland Yard was the headquarters of the police in London, England.

King Edward VII may have ended the investigation so certain facts didn't spread.

However, this report got lost. Many people suspected a cover-up. The report might have named an important person. Leaders could have hidden it to avoid a scandal.

FAST FACT

Both Vicars and Shackleton were accused of having wild parties.

Stories said some staff held wild parties at Dublin Castle.

Police offered a reward for information about the jewels. But the jewels are still missing. And no one knows who took them.

UNTRUE CLUES

One woman claimed to see the jewels in a vision. She told Vicars to dig in a cemetery. He did. But the jewels weren't there.

People can tour Dublin Castle to learn about its history.

COMPREHENSION QUESTIONS

Write your answers on a separate piece of paper.

1. Write a few sentences describing the main ideas of Chapter 1.

2. Which theory about who took the jewels seems the most likely to you? Why?

3. Who was in charge of Dublin Castle's treasure?

   A. Ernest Shackleton

   B. Arthur Vicars

   C. John Kane

4. Why might police think the thief worked at the castle?

   A. The thief used a key.

   B. The thief broke the safe.

   C. The thief left no clues.

5. What does removed mean in this book?

And a ribbon was left in the safe. The thief had removed it from the jewels.

    A. took something off
    B. put something on
    C. burned something up

6. What does security mean in this book?

Police found problems with the castle's security. Earlier that summer, doors had been found unlocked.

    A. work to make something free
    B. efforts to keep something safe
    C. time to go to sleep

Answer key on page 32.

GLOSSARY

aristocrats

People from a high class, often people who are rich or royal.

cemetery

A place where dead people are buried.

collar

A chain or band worn around the neck.

intruder

Someone who goes where they're not allowed.

investigated

Tried to find out the truth about something.

monarchy

A country's royal family, including the king or queen.

motive

A reason for doing something.

scandal

An event that upsets people, often because of bad actions.

suspect

A person the police think may be guilty of a crime.

TO LEARN MORE

BOOKS

Blevins, Wiley. *Ireland*. New York: Scholastic, 2018.

Huddleston, Emma. *Historical Site Bucket List*. Minneapolis: Abdo Publishing, 2022.

Jazynka, Kitson. *History's Mysteries: Curious Clues, Cold Cases, and Puzzles from the Past*. Washington, DC: National Geographic, 2017.

ONLINE RESOURCES

Visit www.apexeditions.com to find links and resources related to this title.

ABOUT THE AUTHOR

Ashley Gish earned her degree in creative writing from Minnesota State University, Mankato. She has authored more than 60 juvenile nonfiction books. Ashley lives happily in Rochester, Minnesota, with her husband, daughter, dog, cat, and three chickens.

INDEX

ANSWER KEY:

1. Answers will vary; 2. Answers will vary; 3. B; 4. A; 5. A; 6. B